GERMAN REMOTE-CONTROL TANK UNITS 1940-1943

Markus Jaugitz

translated from the German by David Johnston

Borgward B I mine-clearance vehicle with three-part roller trailer.

Schiffer Military/Aviation History
Atglen, PA

FOREWORD

The remote-control tank units within the German Panzer Arm have received scant mention in the many publications on the subject to appear in recent years. Since these units, which were classified as secret special formations, never grew beyond battalion size and were usually subordinated to larger units for only brief periods, investigations in the extensive stocks of files held in German and foreign archives proved extremely difficult.

After years of research, the author has succeeded in compiling an almost complete picture of the operational history as well as the organization and equipment of the individual remote-control tank units.

At this point thanks are due to the many former members of the remote-control tank units who were always ready to answer my questions and readily make available their personal papers and photographs. Without their contribution and assistance this publication would not have been possible.

A full description of the technical equipment and armament of the units and their operational histories would require more than a single volume.

This first volume, therefore, deals exclusively with the story of the birth of the remote-control tank units in the years from 1940 to 1943. A second volume, will document the period from 1943-1945.

The author is grateful for any additional material or corrections:

Markus Jaugitz, Max-Joseph-Str.32, 68187 Mannheim.

Borgward B IV heavy explosive charge carrier Model A (Sd.Kfz.301).

Sources

Author's archive
Thomas L. Jentz Archive
Freiburg Military Archive
Archive of the Bovington Tank Museum, Great Britain
National Archives, USA
Deutsche Dienststelle (WAST), Berlin
Army Service Manuals

Photo Sources

Fritz Trenkle Archive
Archive of the NSU Firm
Sonder-Kfz. 301 — Technical Description and Operating Instructions
Author's photo archive

Translated from the German by David Johnston.

Printed in China.
ISBN: 0-7643-0178-0

This book was originally published under the title,
Waffen Arsenal-Die Deutsche Fernlenktruppe 1940-1943
by Podzun-Pallas Verlag

We are interested in hearing from authors with book ideas on related topics.

Published by Schiffer Publishing Ltd.
77 Lower Valley Road
Atglen, PA 19310
Phone: (610) 593-1777
FAX: (610) 593-2002
Please write for a free catalog.
This book may be purchased from the publisher.
Please include $2.95 postage.
Try your bookstore first.

INTRODUCTION

The rapid development of radio telegraphy resulted in the first experiments in remote control by radio being carried out at the beginning of the Twentieth Century.

In Germany the firms of Siemens-Schuckert and Siemens respectively began testing wireless remote-control torpedoes and wire-guided motor boats. As well tests were planned with the remote control of aircraft.

After the outbreak of the First World War, representatives of the Ministry of War decreed that work on the difficult problem of the remote control of aircraft would halt for the time being and that research would concentrate on the simpler remote control of boats.

In the years that followed, extensive tests were carried out in the Kaiser's Germany with remote-control boats, radio-controlled torpedoes and wire-guided glider-bombs and torpedo gliders.

The cease-fire of 1918 was followed by the Treat of Versailles, the provisions of which prohibited further tests with radio-control equipment.

Military interest was reawakened as a result of steady progress in the field of civilian radio technology. In the mid-1930s both the British and French Armies took up the idea of using remote-control tracked vehicles. In 1937 the French career officer and inventor Pommelet produced plans for a small tank, an explosives carrier; it was to be guided toward a suitable target by remote control and its explosive charge detonated there. In military circles this invention was dubbed the "land torpedo."

It was not until 1939 that the German side became involved in the development of radio-controlled vehicles. The Ordnance Department's plans called for the development of an unmanned tracked vehicle. Practical testing revealed unsuspected operational potential and resulted in the development and manufacture of special vehicles which the field forces dubbed "exploding tanks."

The prototype of the Véhicule Pommelet, "VP" for short, was tested at the French troop training grounds Camp de Frileuse in spring 1939. By the end of April 1940, 2,000 examples had been ordered by the French Army, however only 11 were built by the time of the cease-fire. According to a British report, some of the completed "VP"s were successfully used against German tanks near Sedan in May 1940.

ORGANIZATION AND OPERATIONAL USE

The thorough testing of this new type of equipment required the formation of a special unit. The German remote-control tank force was founded in 1940 with the creation of a single company, the 1st Mine-Clearance Company.

From it this special force grew by the end of the war to several battalions and independent companies.

Numerous changes, reorganizations and redesignations took place in the early years between mid-1940 and the beginning of 1943. The following is a list of significant dates and information:

June 1940
Formation of the 1st Mine-Clearance Company. For reasons of secrecy the unit was given the code name "Glienicke Company."

December 1940/May 1941
Expansion of the company into the 1st Mine-Clearance Battalion. The battalion consisted of a battalion headquarters and two mine-clearance companies.

Equipment trials in occupied France in the area around its new base at Weißenburg, Alsace.

May/June 1940
Transfer of the battalion to East Prussia and preparations in the operations area.

June/July
Three-week tour of duty in the area of Army Group Center with the VIII and XXXIX Army Corps. Subsequent transfer back to Germany to the base at Wünsdorf.

September 1941
Renamed 300th Panzer Battalion and transferred to Cottbus.

February 1942
Renamed 300th Panzer Battalion (FL); formation of 3rd Company. The battalion consisted of a battalion headquarters, a headquarters company, two companies with radio-controlled equipment (1st and 2nd Companies) and one with wire-guided equipment (3rd Company). (FL = Remote Control)

Below: The kleine Panzerbefehlswagen, or small armored command vehicle (Sd.Kfz.265), served as control tank for the mine-clearance vehicles. Here a control tank of the 1st Mine-Clearance Company drives past a parked Borgward B I during an exercise in occupied France.

May 1942
Formation of a Panzer Experimental and Training Company (FL), as well as a Panzer Field Replacement Company (FL) by the 5th Panzer Replacement Battalion at Neuruppin.

Transfer of the 300th Panzer Battalion (FL) to the Eastern Front.

June 1942
Operational use of the battalion in the conquest of the fortress of Sevastopol on the crimean Peninsula as part of the 11th Army.

July/August 1942
Formation of the Tropical Test Detachment (FL) with one platoon each of radio-controlled and wire-guided equipment and subsequent transfer to the North African theater.

Combat duty by the 300th Panzer Battalion (FL) with the 1st Panzer Army during the fighting in the Donets Basin and the Battle of Rostov. Subsequently transferred into the Leningrad area.

September/November 1942
300th Panzer Battalion (FL) renamed the 301st Panzer Battalion and reorganized near the front.

September/November 1942
Formation of the 300th Panzer Replacement Battalion (Fkl) at Neuruppin with battalion headquarters, one panzer replacement company and one instruction and experimental company. (Fkl = radio-controlled.)

Combat duty by the 301st Panzer Battalion in the area of the 11th and 18th Armies. Individual component elements of the battalion transferred back to Arnswalde.

1st Company, 301st Panzer Battalion transferred to the southern sector and took part in the defensive fighting at the Don, in the Kalmuck Steppe and in the Donets Region.

January 1943
The 300th Panzer Replacement Battalion (Fkl) renamed 300th (FKL) Panzer Replacement Battalion and moved to the base at Eisenach.

The battalion was organized into a battalion headquarters, a panzer experimental and instruction company (1./Pz.Ers.Abt. (Fkl) 300), two light panzer training companies (Fkl) (2./ and 3./Pz.Ers.Abt. (Fkl) 300) and a replacement company (4./Pz.Ers.Abt. (Fkl) 300).

February 1943
1st Company, 301st Panzer Battalion and the Tropical Test Detachment (FL) transferred back to Eisenach.

This converted Panzerkampfwagen III Ausf. J served as a control tank with the 1st Company of the 300th Panzer Battalion. Here it has been loaded onto a flatcar for transport from the northern sector of the Eastern Front. Some of the crew are wearing the reversible grey-white winter sits introduced at the end of 1942.

VEHICLE DESCRIPTIONS

B I MINE-CLEARANCE VEHICLE

On 21 November 1939 the Borgward Company of Bremen received a contract from the Ordnance Department to build fifty special fully-tracked vehicles. These were foreseen as tractors for a three-part roller trailer and were to be used in the remote-control mode for the clearance of mines. The vehicle's official designation was Mine-Clearance Vehicle B I (Sd.Kfz.300). As it was assumed that the vehicle would have a very brief service life, no great costs were to e involved in its manufacture. To meet the requirement Borgward built a fully-tracked tractor with a concrete superstructure.

The chassis consisted of a rectangular hull, in the rear of which a Borgward Type 4 M 1.5 R II 4-cylinder, carburetor engine was installed. A driveshaft extended forward from the engine and ended in an electro-magnetic single-disc chain drive. A connecting shaft extended from the gearbox left and right into the reduction gear units. The reduction gear units were flange-mounted on the exterior of the hull's low sidewalls.

Between the twelve-tooth drive sprocket and the idler wheel there were three large roadwheels on each side. One special feature of these roadwheels was that they dispensed with the solid rubber tires used by most armored vehicles in favor of four-piece wooden tires. Just above the hull began the cast concrete superstructure which protected the engine, transmission, fuel tank and remote-control. Speed was controlled by means of a large lever installed on the left side of the vehicle. There was the stop position as well as settings for 2 and 5 kilometers per hour. Just behind this lever there was an opening through which the exhaust pipe was led outside.

The tactical emblem of the 1st Mine-Clearance Company and, as of 1941, of the headquarters of the 1st Mine-Clearance Battalion. The rhombus stands for tank, the circle for mine-clearance roller.

This ended in a muffler which was installed horizontally above the last roadwheel.

A sheet steel framework was set into the upper part of the concrete superstructure and was covered by a rectangular maintenance hatch. In the left rear corner of the maintenance hatch there was a shielded ventilation opening.

Deliveries of the 1.5-ton vehicles took place between January and May 1940, however at that time the fifty vehicles still lacked the necessary radio remote control.

All Borgward B Is were delivered to the newly-formed 1st Mine-Clearance Company. These carried out extensive clearances in the remaining French minefields in front of the Maginot Line, in the course of which the majority of all B Is were expended.

Below: The cog-like elements of the roller trailer were supposed to explode buried mines when they rolled over them. This B I has no markings.

This mine-clearance tank drove over a mine during a demonstration. The right track was blown off and the maintenance hatch tossed to the side.

Below: Vehicle number 30 in difficult terrain. The purpose of the rags was to facilitate optical tracking of the vehicle, since during the guidance procedure it was often out of sight behind hills or in defiles.

Above and below:
The interior of this B I mine-clearance tank contained an explosive charge. When the vehicle ran over a mine the forward part of the concrete superstructure was destroyed together with the track and running gear. Clearly visible is the placement of the transmission and the 4-cylinder Borgward carburetor engine.

On 3 April 1940 a follow-up order for 100 special vehicles was given to the Borgward Company. They were designated Type B II and retained the Sd.Kfz. Number 300. A number of improvements were made compared to the B I.

The chassis was lengthened and the number of roadwheels increased to four per side. The reduction gear units and the drive sprockets were installed in a higher position. The tracks, which rose sharply to the drive sprockets, were led over a return roller located at the hull's midway point above the second and third roadwheels.

Changes in the chassis and superstructure resulted in an increase in the weight of the B II to 2.3 tons, which made necessary the installation of a more powerful power plant, the Borgward Type 6 M 2.3 RTBV carburetor engine.

While the speed-control lever remained on the left side of the vehicle, the muffler was now installed at the rear on the upper end of the superstructure. The ventilation openings were also placed in the vehicle's rear end, shielded by horizontally-mounted steel strips. There were still several maintenance hatches on the top side of the B II which provided access to the engine compartment and to the transmission.

All 100 B IIs, production of which began in July 1940, were issued to the 1st Mine-Clearance Battalion.

However, the mine-clearance battalion employed the B II, not as a tractor for the roller-trailer, but for special experiments "for purposes not originally intended"; it was in the course of similar tests that the majority of the B Is had been lost.

Since the mine-clearance vehicles with towed roller-trailers had failed to achieve the desired success, the idea was born to equip the special vehicles with a large explosive charge and steer them by remote control into a minefield. If a vehicle drove over a mine, the explosion set off the explosive charge in the interior of the vehicle. As a rule, the resulting shock wave exploded all the mines buried in the vicinity by means of sympathetic detonation.

In the course of the testing the question arose how to employ radio-controlled explosives carriers against other targets such as bunkers and concrete or steel obstacles, but also against armored vehicles. Development of a new detonation method was required. This problem was solved by boring a hole in the concrete superstructure above the left drive sprocket, which was used to install a metal rail across the front of the vehicle. If the B II drove into an obstacle, the rail was driven backward and set off the detonation mechanism.

Both detonation methods were tested during operations in Russia by the 1st Mine-Clearance Battalion in summer 1941.

The B II proved generally unsatisfactory in service. Difficulties with the makeshift detonation mechanism, countless technical faults in the special vehicles and constant trouble with the radio-control equipment, which was sensitive and very prone to failure, prevented a continuation of the mine-clearing mission.

Below: In contrast to the B I, the Borgward B II mine-clearance tank had four large roadwheels and a return roller on each side.

Above:
Members of the 2nd Company of the 1st Mine-Clearance Battalion with a brand-new Borgward B II. The hitch for towing the roller trailer was positioned low on the rear of the chassis.

Left:
This photo illustrates the size of the Borgward B II. The driver has placed the speed-control lever in the "stop position."

This mine-clearance tank of the 2nd Company, 1st Mine-Clearance Battalion is equipped with the modified detonation mechanism. This system did not prove a success.

Below: The B IIs of the 1st Company, 1st Mine-Clearance Battalion which were employed in the attack on Russia soon bogged down in the swampy and muddy terrain and had to be recovered.

A Borgward B II during the advance on Minsk, late June 1941. A platoon of the 2nd Company, 1st Mine-Clearance Battalion was subordinated to the 58th Armored Engineer Battalion (7th Panzer Division), the rest of the company to the 20th Panzer Division.

Several mine-clearance tanks and control tanks of the 2nd Company, 1st Mine-Clearance Battalion after breaking through the frontier positions during the attack on the town of Kalvaria on 22 June 1941.

The Ordnance Office also gave the Borgward Company a contract to develop an amphibious version of the B II.

According to information provided by three former members of the 1st Mine-Clearance Battalion, there were three amphibious B IIs. The vehicles were given the name "Ente", or "Duck", by the unit.

Structurally the vehicle was almost identical to the B II, however the roadwheels were solid. The vehicle also lacked return rollers between the second and third roadwheels.

Instead of the concrete superstructure, a sheet steel floating body was mounted on the chassis hull. On top of the vehicle there was a superstructure, which was designed so that it could be removed quickly for maintenance purposes. The end section of the exhaust pipe projected up and out from the rear of the vehicle.

The vehicle was propelled through the water by a boat propeller, steering was by means of two rudders. The propeller and rudder blades were installed centrally on the rear of the vehicle.

2nd Company of the 1st Mine-Clearance Battalion tested the "Ente" in a tributary of the Rhine River under conditions of great secrecy in spring 1941. The vehicles were later used in action in July 1941 during the crossing of the Dvina River.

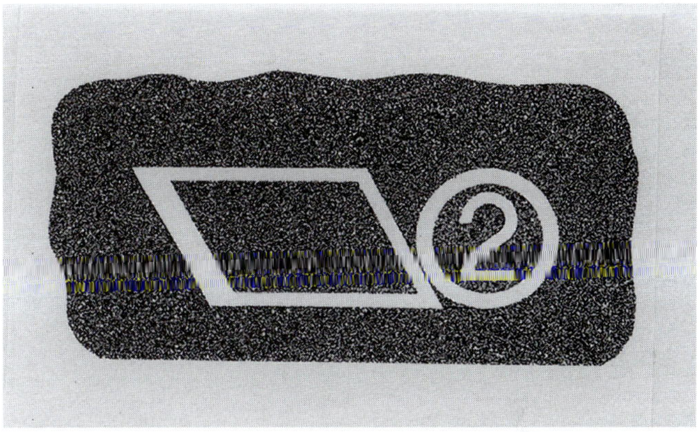

Tactical emblem of the 2nd Company, 1st Mine-Clearance Battalion, later of the 2nd Company, 300th Panzer Battalion (FL).

Below:
The amphibious version of the Borgward B II. Unlike the standard version this vehicle had solid roadwheels. Positioned at the rear were the propeller and the rudder blades, which propelled and steered the "Ente" through the water.

B III MINE-CLEARANCE VEHICLE

No information exists on the B III.

There must have been a prototype, which in late June-early July 1941 was transported by rail from the Borgward Company in Bremen to the Eastern Front. When the 1st Mine-Clearance Battalion was transferred back to Germany the B III was taken to the unit's new base at Wünsdorf and tested there.

The B III is said to have been structurally similar to the B II apart from having a concrete superstructure instead of a metal one.

Above and below:
Each mine-clearance company had 10 small armored command vehicles. These served as control tanks for the mine-clearance tanks. As well as having an additional antenna and the command transmitter set, these vehicles had a panoramic telescope mounted in the roof, the same as that installed in the turret of the Panzerkampfwagen 38 t.

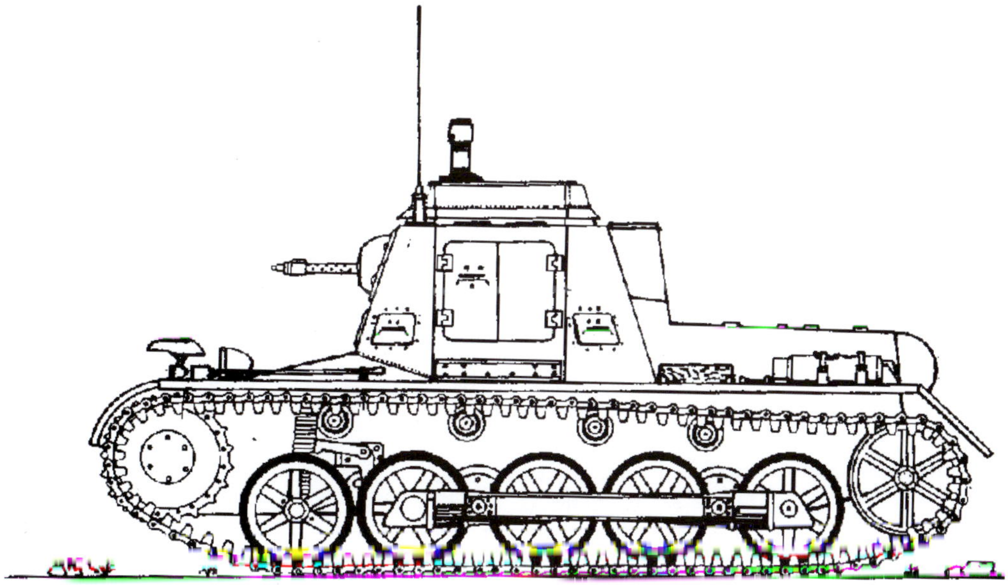

Kleiner Panzerbefehlswagen (small armored command vehicle, Sd.Kfz.265). Used as control tank by the 1st Mine-Clearance Battalion, summer 1941.

A small armored command vehicle of the 2nd Company, 1st Mine-Clearance Battalion near Vilna shortly after the start of the campaign against Russia. Five Sd.Kfz. 265s were handed over to the headquarters of Armored Group 3 before the battalion was withdrawn in July 1941.

As early as autumn 1941 the 1st Mine-Clearance Battalion had an NSU Kettenkrad modified to serve as an experimental remote-control vehicle. The vehicle's driver's seat and all the steering controls had been moved to the rear of the vehicle. The sidewalls were raised and the free space around the transmission was prepared to accept an explosive charge. The vehicle was intended to fill the same operational role as the Borgward B II mine-clearance vehicle.

In spring 1942 the NSU Company, with the cooperation of the 300th Panzer Battalion (FL), developed a radio-controlled explosives carrier based on the Kettenkrad, in the process of which the following changes were carried out. The same command receiver was installed in the Kettenkrad as in the B IV Heavy Explosives Carrier. A locking mechanism was installed between the steering fork and the vehicle hull. The engine cowling was higher and designed as a single unit which could be completely removed for maintenance work. The rear section of the Kettenkrad was totally redesigned. In place of the rear seat a special housing was attached, in which the non-jettisonable explosive charge was located.

The NSU explosives carrier was driven to the starting position by its driver and there turned 180 degrees. The front fork was then locked in place and the drive mechanism switched to radio remote-control. The vehicle was guided to the target in reverse gear and was destroyed when the explosive charge was set off at the target.

Because of its jerky motion while under radio remote-control, in 1942 the vehicle was dubbed the "Springer" ("jumper") by the men of the 300th Panzer Battalion (FL). At least four of these vehicles were used in the Battle of Sevastopol in June 1942.

The NSU explosives carrier proved unsatisfactory in action. Due to the shifting of weight and the narrow wheelbase, the Kettenkrads often tipped over in the hilly terrain of the area of operations in the Crimea.

Above and below:
First prototype of a remote-control NSU Kettenkrad. The driver's seat was moved to the rear of the vehicle and the superstructure was raised.

Above and below:
The second model of the remote-control NSU Kettenkrad. The photos were taken when the vehicle was delivered by NSU in Neckarsulm. The canister mount on the rear was later removed. While the vehicle was being driven the locking rods were fastened to the front fork on the left and right.

Tracked elements of the 300th Panzer Battalion (FL) en route to the Crimea by train. There are two remote-control Kettenkrad in front of and behind each Panzer III.

Below: This remote-control Kettenkrad is being serviced in the battalion's assembly area. The engine cowling was completely removed and placed on the explosives compartment.

Above:
This command tank has suffered track damage. In difficult country the remote-control Kettenkrad was often used as a supply vehicle as well. In contrast to the Borgward B IV, the Kettenkrads had a WH number plate (WH = Armed Forces Army).

Left:
A remote-control NSU Kettenkrad during a rest stop in the advance on Rostov in July 1942.

Based on experience gained with the mine-clearance vehicles, the Ordnance Department requested the development of a remote-control heavy explosive charge carrier. In October 1941 the Borgward Company was charged with the design of such a vehicle, which received the designation B IV. The heavy explosive charge carrier was to be guided unmanned to its target, jettison a large explosive charge there, and be withdrawn before the latter exploded. In addition to its role as explosive charge carrier, the B IV could also be used for reconnaissance and smoke-laying missions.

Production began in April 1942 and the first fifteen vehicles were delivered to the 300th Panzer Battalion (FL) that same month. The B IV received the Sd.Kfz. Number 301. The vehicle had a combat weight of 3.6 tons and was powered by a Borgward six-cylinder Type 6 M 2.3 RTBV carburetor motor. Its off-road capability was equivalent to that of the Panzer III. With a full tank of fuel (123 liters) range was approximately 200 kilometers, maximum speed was 38 kilometers per hour.

The jettisonable explosive charge weighed 450 kg. The explosive used in the charge was relatively safe to handle. This meant that when the detonator was not installed, the charge could be struck by small-caliber projectiles without exploding. If a B IV caught fire the charge burned slowly away.

In addition to the explosive charge, a smoke generator could be installed on the B IV. Eight Type 42 Long Smoke Candles could either be jettisoned and ignited or ignited on the moving B IV without being jettisoned, in both cases by radio command. The Type 42 smoke candle produced smoke for 25 to 30 minutes. As well, eight decontamination projectiles or eight containers of decontamination agent could be fired in place of the smoke candles. After release the decontamination agent spread and created a decontaminated island for a group of two or three men. The latter was never used in action, however.

While on the road the heavy explosive charge carrier was steered by hand by a driver; in contrast, in action it was guided by radio, unmanned, from a control tank. In the control tank was the signal transmitter with antenna and command sender, while in the B IV was the command receiver. The following commands could be executed by radio: "start, stop, right, left, faster, slower, forward, backward, detonate, jettison, and make smoke." All of these commands were received by the command receiver in the explosive charge carrier and transmitted to the oil control unit, which transformed the signals into mechanical force.

In the beginning there was only a small windscreen in front of the driver's position. Following heavy casualties among drivers in the first actions involving the B IV, the vehicle was retrofitted with a folding, three-part shield which protected the driver against bullets and shrapnel.

A total of 628 of the A-Model of the B IV Heavy Explosive Charge Carrier were built from April 1942 to June 1943, 12 of which were pre-production test vehicles. Alone 390 vehicles were built in a special program between the beginning of February and the end of June 1943.

Borgward B IV heavy explosives carrier prior to operations against Russian field positions in front of Fortress Sevastopol. Note the windshield, which offered the driver no protection.

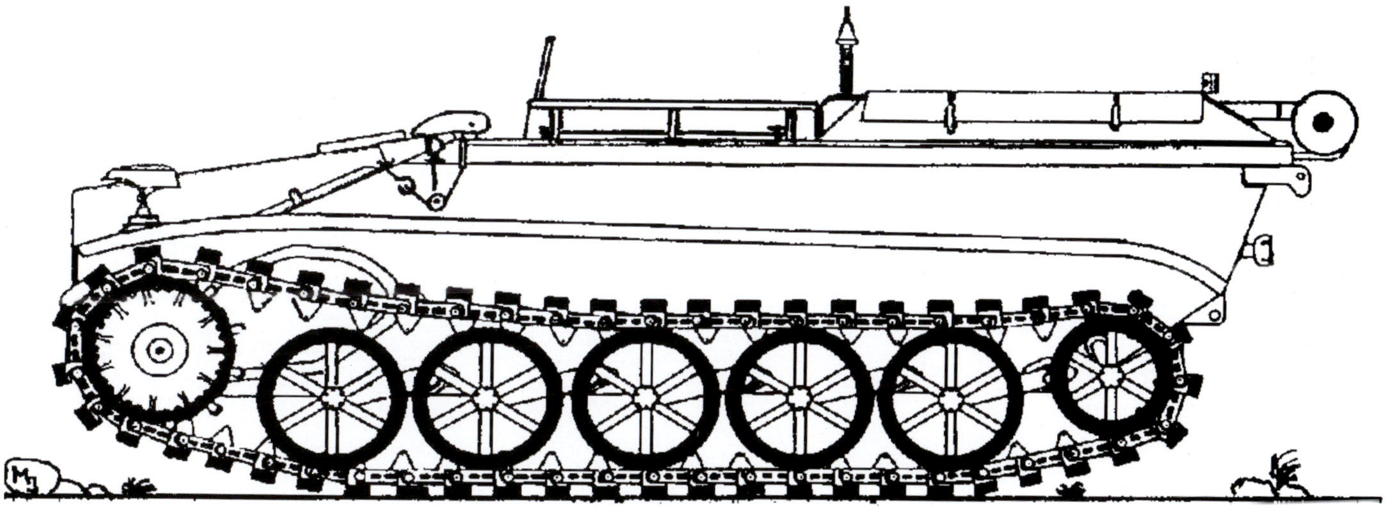

Borgward B IV Model A Heavy Explosives Carrier — initial version

This Borgward B IV has released its explosives container. Inside it was 450 kg of ecrasite. This was pressed into shape and filled the entire container. The detonator with delay pellet was inserted in the rear center of the charge.

Right and below left: Side-views of the Borgward Type 6 M 2.3 RTBV six-cylinder carburetor motor. This motor had previously powered the B II. Its maximum output was 49 H.P., displacement was 2,242 cubic centimeters.

Below:
The transmission of the B IV comprised two two-speed transmissions coupled one behind the other. Both transmissions were flange-mounted to the steering drive in a common housing. The first transmission had one forward and one reverse gear, the second two forward gears. This provided four possible gear selections.

Right:
FuKS 8 radio-control transmitter set for ultra-shortwave guidance of explosives carriers.

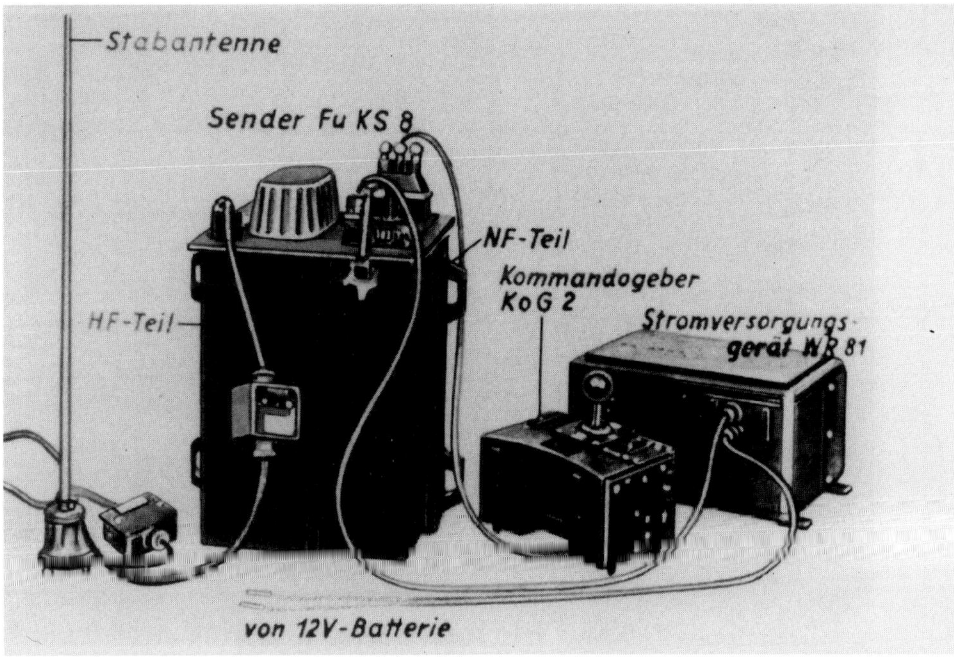

Each of he Borgward B IV's two tracks consisted of 50 Type Kgw 53 200/140 track links. The links were held together by bolts, one the one side by an head, on the other side by an hexagonal head with washer. Each track link had a rubber pad which was held in place by two bolts.

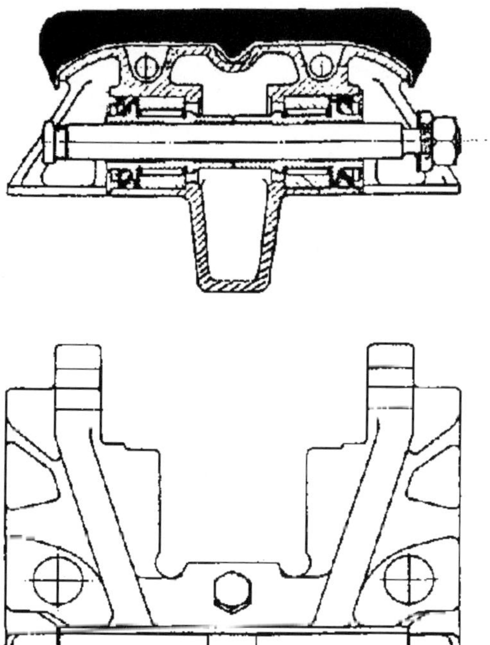

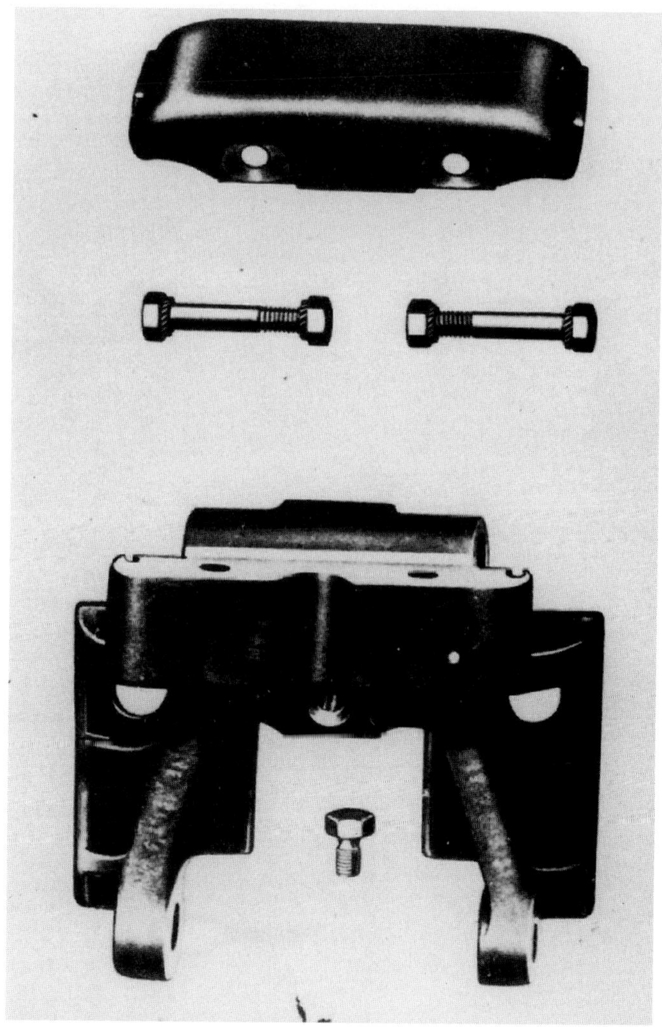

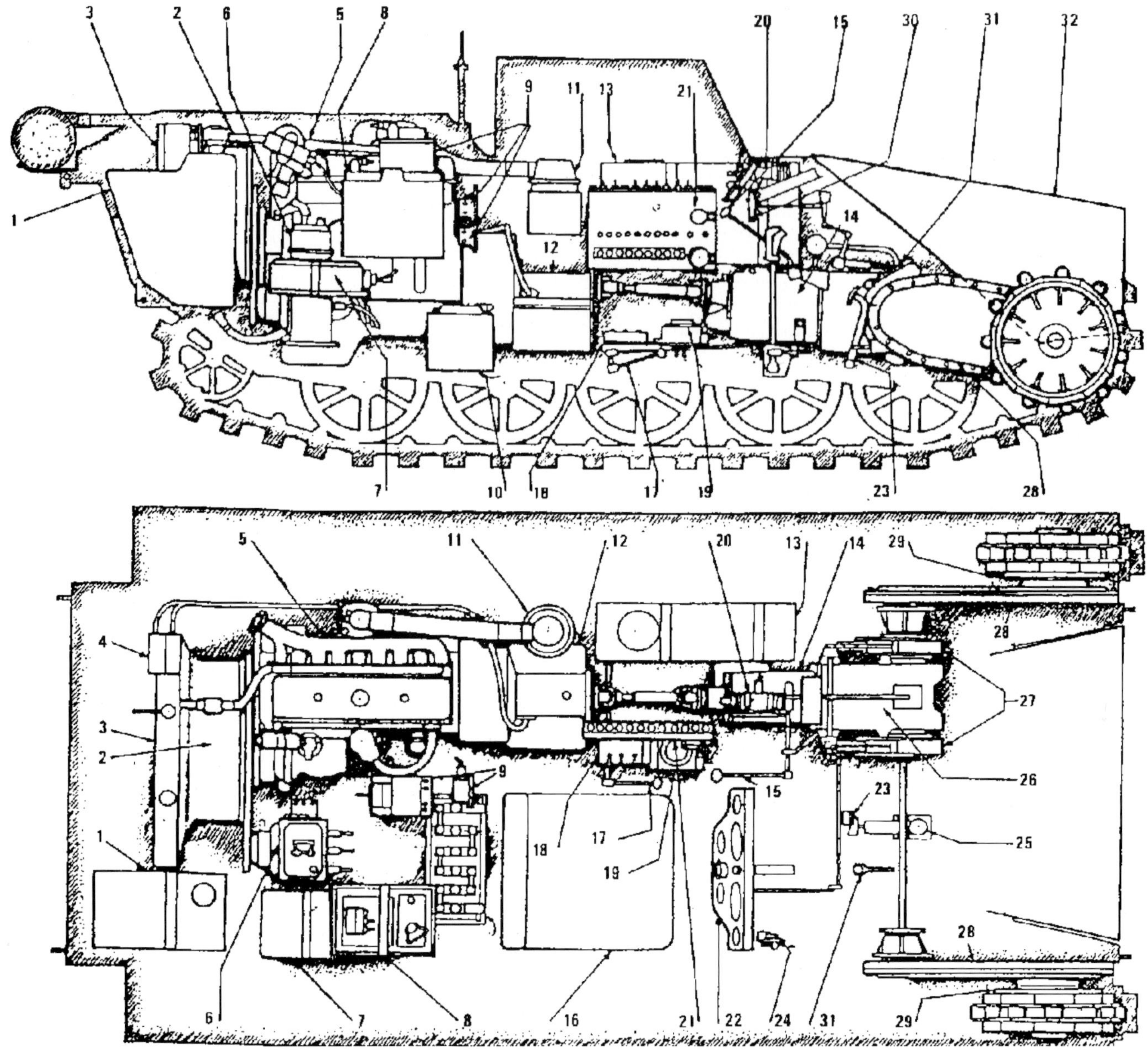

1. Fuel tank 95 liters
2. Fan housing
3. Radiator
4. Oil cooler for hydraulic coupling
5. 6-cylinder Borgward carburetor motor
6. Hydraulic steering device
7. Electrical converter
8. Command receiver
9. Relay box
10. Vehicle battery
11. Air filter
12. Hydraulic coupling
13. Fuel tank 28 liters
14. Transmission
15. Shift lever road/off-road
16. Driver's seat
17. Shift lever forward/reverse
18. Detonator battery
19. Detonator pre-selector
20. Main hydraulic cylinder
21. Main control box
22. Instrument panel
23. Foot brake
24. Hand brake
25. Master brake cylinder
26. Differential housing
27. Steering brakes
28. Reduction gear housing
29. Vehicle brakes
30. Shift lever
31. Gas pedal
32. Jettisonable explosives container

Left:
A Borgward B IV of the 2nd Company, 300th Panzer Battalion (FL) on a train e route to the Crimea. The panel lying to the right of the driver's seat was used to cover the driver's compartment and the instruments.

Below:
Dispersed in terrain, the B IV drivers await their operational orders. The explosive charge in the jettisonable container was not "armed" until just before the vehicles moved off.

Motorcycles enabled the mechanics of the repair echelons to reach broken-down vehicles quickly and carry out the necessary repairs.

Below: In order to better camouflage the tanks and special vehicles in the terrain of the Crimea, a thin brew of powdered lime and water was often mixed and crudely applied to the vehicles with brooms and brushes.

The radio equipment installed in the first B IVs was very prone to break down. The repair echelons were often forced to make frequency adjustments — usually just before the vehicles went into action.

Below: In the shelter of a sunken road three Borgward B IVs of the 1st Company, 330th Panzer Battalion (FL) prepare for an attack. As soon as the vehicles reached their starting position, the drivers climbed out and switched to remote-control mode.

A heavy explosives carrier rolls past an overturned Russian T 26 tank. There were tank-versus-tank battles in front of Sevastopol, in which the control tanks of the 300th Panzer Battalion (FL) also took part.

Below: The control tanks provided supporting fire while the B IVs advanced on their targets, taking out enemy anti-tank guns employed against the explosives carriers.

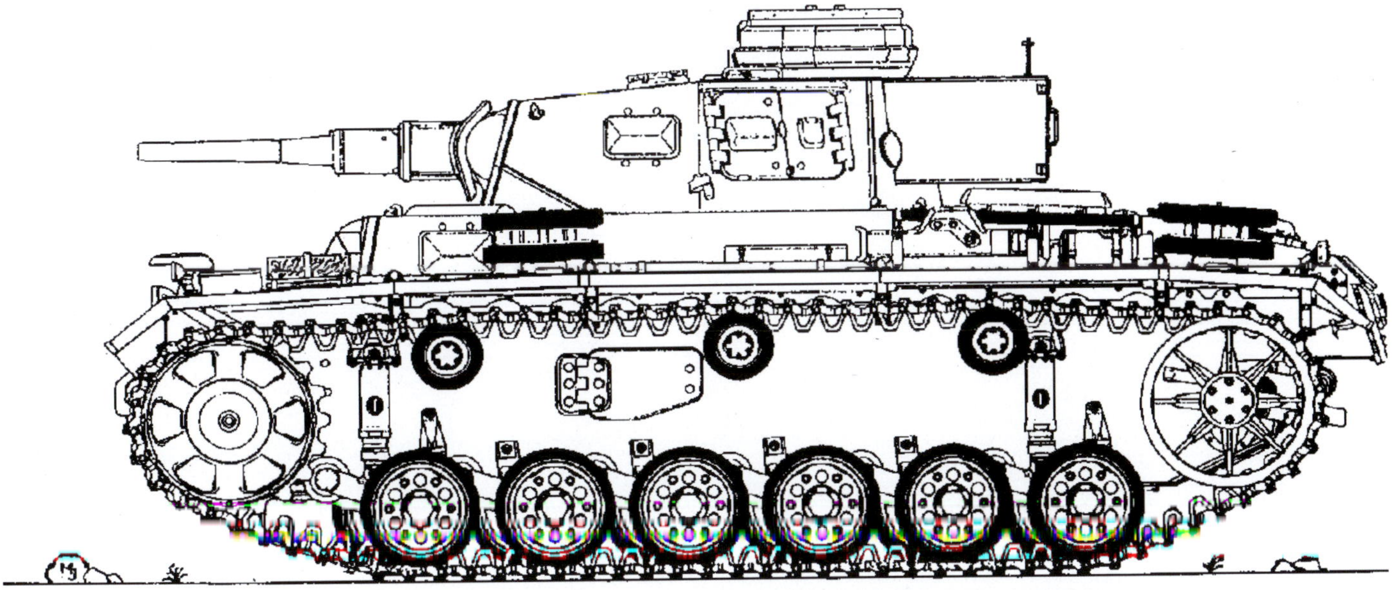

Panzerkampfwagen III Model J in use as control tank by the 300th Panzer Battalion (FL), May 1942.

Panzerkampfwagen III Model J of the 1st Company, 300th Panzer Battalion (FL). An equipment box was mounted behind the turret; in it was installed the command transmitter and other radio equipment.

A lightly-camouflaged control tank on the move. Note the muzzle cover, which protected the gun against dust and dirt. The wooden box on the right fender was a feature of all control tanks and was used to store personal items.

Below: The first B IVs had two small headlights in addition to the Notek headlight on the left fender. In front of the windshield is the protective hood which shielded the fuse placement opening.

A remote-control squad in readiness position. Four explosives carriers were subordinated to one command tank. The command set could guide two B IVs to the target simultaneously.

Below:
This B IV had its left track blown off by a mine during the Battle of Sevastopol. Normally the explosion should have set off the 450 kgs of explosives and thus destroyed the damaged vehicle. This was intended to prevent any B IV from falling into enemy hands.

Left:
Tactical symbol of the 1st Company, 1st Mine-Clearance Battalion and later the 1st Company, 300th Panzer Battalion (FL). The symbol was applied on the front and rear of all wheeled and tracked vehicles.

This symbol of the remote-control units has often been mistakenly attributed to the armored units of the "Hermann Göring" Parachute Panzer Division.

A control tank on guard duty in the operational area. In addition to watching over the explosive carrier missions, the tanks of the 300th Panzer Battalion (FL) destroyed 36 bunkers and 11 guns during the fighting at Sevastopol and sank a coastal patrol vessel.

The engine access panels of this heavy explosives carrier have been completely removed. In this way the mechanics could carry out the necessary work in the engine compartment unhindered.

Below: The 1st Company was one of the first units to reach the harbor of the hotly-contested fortress on 1 July 1942. A total of 37 B IV remote-control missions were carried out in the course of the fighting at Sevastopol. Meanwhile all the tanks received black turret numbers.

Left:
This B IV was correctly loaded for rail transport. Maintaining the rubber-blocked running gear was very time consuming. Lost or damaged blocks had to be replaced immediately. Therefore the units soon called for a vehicle with non-lubricated running gear.

Below:
This explosives carrier is ready for a remote-control mission. The driver has left the vehicle and the command tank has assumed control. The distance between the command tank and the B IV could not exceed 2,000 meters. If this distance was exceeded, the B IV's receiver automatically switched to "stop."

"STROLCH", a platoon leader's tank of the 2nd Company, 300th Panzer Battalion (FL), in Tolle, Crimea in June 1942.

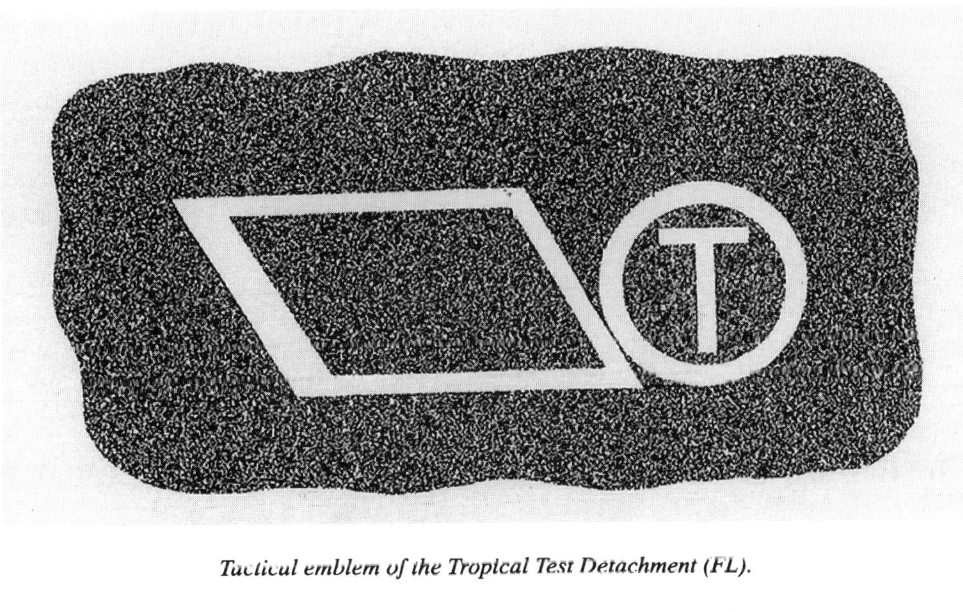

Tactical emblem of the Tropical Test Detachment (FL).

The Tropical Test Detachment (FL) carried out extensive tests near Benghazi with one platoon of B IV heavy explosive charge carriers and one of "Goliath" light explosive charge carriers. This Panzer III Ausf. J command tank wears additional armor plate, which was mainly seen on the later "J" model with the long 50mm KwK 39/L60 gun.

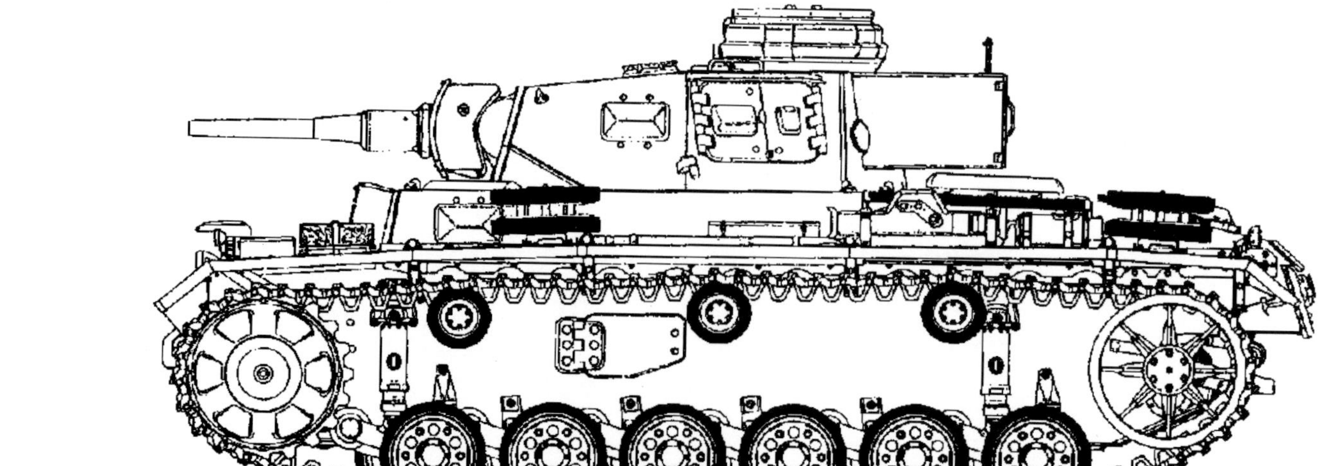

Panzerkampfwagen III Model J with additional armor serving as a command tank with the Tropical Test Detachment (FL).

A B IV of the Tropical Test Detachment (FL) on the move. Tests involving the remote-control operation of the explosive charge carrier in the African theater were mostly negative, as setting frequencies was extremely difficult and the vehicles did not react to the command signals.

Below:
One of the three command tanks of the B IV platoon. All of the test detachment's Panzer IIIs were handed over to the headquarters of Panzer Army Africa before the unit was withdrawn.

Above and below:
The Borgward B IVs of the 301st Panzer Battalion could not be used in the winter of 1942-43 in front of Leningrad as their hydraulic steering systems failed in sub-zero temperatures. The hydraulic steering systems converted radio signals into mechanical force. If the system failed the vehicle could not be remotely controlled.

Company commander's tank 1st Company, 301st Panzer Battalion. This Panzerkampfwagen Ausf. L has received a washable winter scheme of whitewash over its basic grey finish.

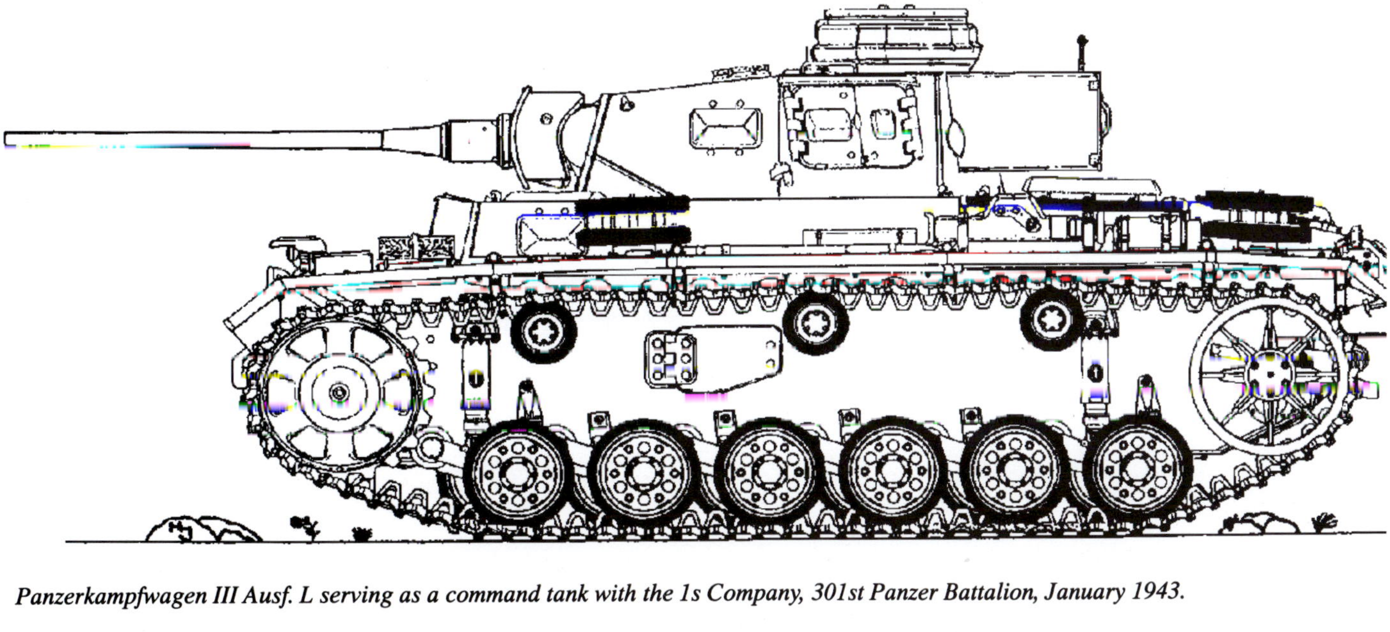

Panzerkampfwagen III Ausf. L serving as a command tank with the 1s Company, 301st Panzer Battalion, January 1943.

Driving school — B IVs of the 300th Panzer Test and Replacement Battalion on the troop training grounds at Berka, Thuringia. The training area was near the unit's base at Eisenach. The Ordnance Department maintained a field office in Berka, where experiments and tests were carried out with newly-developed tracked vehicles. Below: In the spring of 1943 the B IVs of the 2nd and 3rd Training Companies were employed in the driver training role. Including alternate drivers, a remote-control panzer battalion with 108 explosives carriers required approximately 150 B IV drivers.

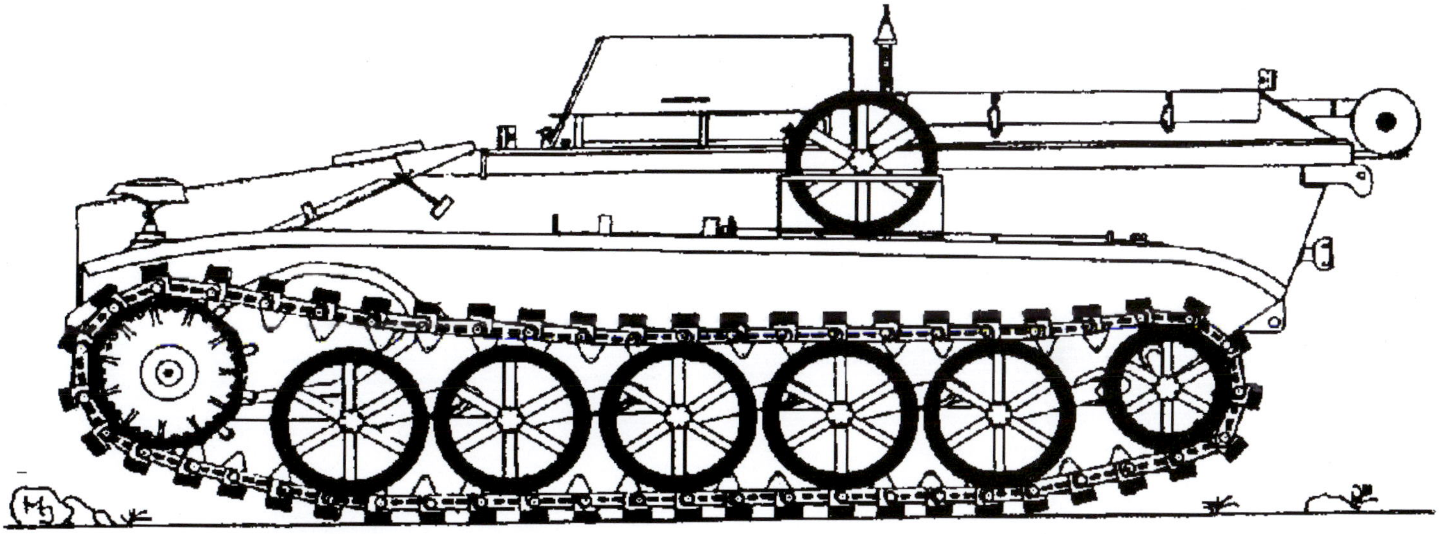

Modified version of a B IV Heavy Explosive Charge Carrier Model A. Note the protection offered the driver, the spare roadwheel, and the modified jettison system for the explosives container.

A "special driver" in his B IV. Located behind the driver in front of the engine cover is the command receiver antenna.

WIRE-GUIDED VEHICLES

"GOLIATH" LIGHT EXPLOSIVE CHARGE CARRIER

At the beginning of 1940 the French inventor Kégresse designed a light caterpillar tractor with rubber tracks. Armed with a small explosive charge, the vehicle was supposed to be guided by wire to obstacles and fortifications and detonated. A test vehicle was sunk in the Seine before the cease-fire at the end of June 1940. It was later recovered and thoroughly examined by German experts.

At the end of June 1940 the Ordnance Department tasked the Borgward Company with the development of an unmanned small tracked vehicle which was to transport an explosive charge weighing approximately 50 kg. The result, after several months of work, was the Small Explosive Charge Carrier (Sd.Kfz.302), which soon came to be known as the "Goliath."

The vehicle was powered by two Bosch electric motors and was guided by wire to its target. Maximum speed was 10 kilometers per hour. In April 1942 the first 15 vehicles from the test series went to the 300th Panzer Battalion (FL). These and other light explosive charge carriers saw action for the first time in the fighting for Sevastopol. The Tropical Test Detachment (FL) evaluated several Sd.Kfz.302s in the North African theater.

Prototype of the Kégresse caterpillar tractor during a demonstration in spring 1940.

Borgward prototype of the "Goliath" Light Explosive Charge Carrier. The explosive charge was located in the steel compartment on the left; in front of it is the drive system and the spool with cable for the wire-guidance system.

Right:
Four men use a transport cart to move a light explosive charge carrier close to the target.

Left:
The 370-kilogram vehicle was then unloaded and armed.

Right:
The "Goliath" sets off and moves toward its target. Located in the front part of the 5-mm armored hull was 60 kg of explosives.

Platoon commander's tank "STROLCH II" of the B IV platoon of the Tropical Test Detachment (FL) in the El Daba quartering area in October 1942.

Below: If the terrain was too difficult, and since the effective range was only 800 meters, the light explosives carriers had to be brought to the starting position by the command tank. Here two "Goliaths" are loaded on a Panzerkampfwagen III.

This light explosive charge carrier has just been unloaded. the hatch over the guide-wire opening is still closed. The broad white stripes on the rear hatch helped the controller in orientation during the remote-control process.

Below: The three-conductor control cable wound off the drum as the vehicle moved. Via this cable the vehicle received the signals "forward, reverse, left, right, stop." This Sd.Kfz. 302 has an additional fairing on the roof of the vehicle, the purpose of which is unknown.

After the end of the campaign in the west in summer 1940 a large number of undamaged vehicles were assigned to many german units for further use. At the end of 1941 the 300th Panzer Battalion received approximately 60 captured tractors of British and Belgian origin.

The vehicles were the English Bren Gun Carrier (Carrier, Bren, No. 2, Mark I) and the Belgian Utility Tractor (Tracteur Chenille Vickers-Carden-Lloyd Utility). Produced under license by the firm of Familleureux, the Belgian vehicles differed from the English original in their size.

All captured armored vehicles were supposed to be employed as wire-guided explosive charge carriers. To this end every cavity in the Bren Gun Carriers and Utility Tractors was filled with explosives. The total weight of explosives was approximately 700 kg. A large cable drum was attached to the rear of the vehicle for the wire control. Control was by means of the same command transmitter that was used in the Sd.Kfz.302.

Both types of captured armored vehicle were used for the first time in the Crimea. In mid-September 1942 the 3rd Company of the 300th Panzer Battalion (FL) still had eight Bren explosive charge carriers on strength.

The use of captured vehicles as explosive charge carriers was not a success. There were frequent mechanical breakdowns when they were used in difficult terrain and at longer ranges. Maintaining and repairing the vehicles proved extremely complicated on account of the poor spares situation. In an operational report dated 22 June 1942, the commanding officer of the 300th Panzer Battalion, Hauptmann Weicke, requested that in future the remote control of captured vehicles should remain a secondary task for the remote-control units.

In addition to the two special vehicles described here, in 1942 and 1943 the 300th Panzer Battalion tested numerous other vehicles for their usability as remote-control explosives carriers. Among them were the VW Schwimmwagen and the French UE Tractor. Unfortunately, so far no documentation has been found concerning these tests and developments.

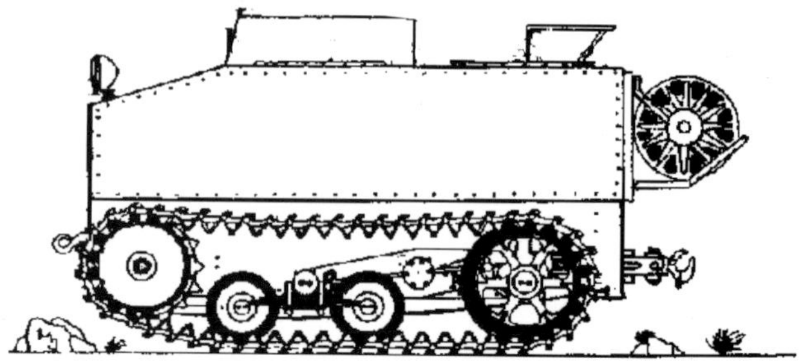

Vickers Utility Tractor converted for use as a wire-guided explosives carrier in service with the 3rd Company, 300th Panzer Battalion (FL), June 1942. Below: The Belgian license-built version of the Carden Lloyd Utility Tractor differed from the original only in the wider wheelbase of the running gear. Here two tractors of the Belgian Army.

Below: A Utility Explosives Carrier in readiness position. This type of explosives carrier was used with success against Soviet field positions on the Sapun Heights in the Crimea.

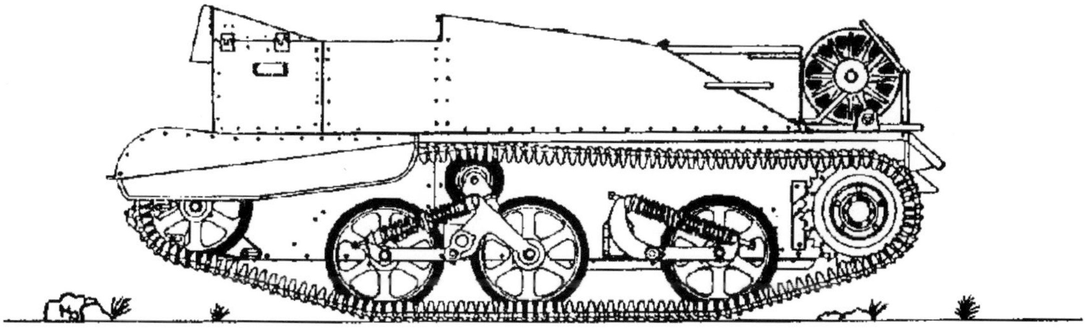

Left:
Bren Carrier converted for use as a wire-guided explosives carrier in service with the 3rd Company, 300th Panzer Battalion (FL), June 1942.

Right:
This Bren Explosives Carrier was employed in the fighting in the city center of Sevastopol. It was hit before reaching its target; the explosive charge burned up without exploding.

Left:
The remaining elements of the 3rd Company, 300th Panzer Battalion (FL) were shipped back to Arnswalde in November 1942. On this vehicle one can see the large cable drum through which the remote-control process was carried out.

The Spielberger German Armor & Military Vehicles Series

Four volumes in the classic series by reknowned German panzer historian Walter Spielberger are now available in new English editions. Known for his emphasis on detail, Spielberger chronicles each production variation and later modifications. Line drawings by Hilary Doyle complement the discussion of each model type.

Size: 8 1/2" x 11" 288 pages hard cover
over 460 photographs
ISBN: 0-88740-397-2 $39.95

Size: 8 1/2" x 11" 256 pages hard cover
over 240 photographs
ISBN: 0-88740-398-0 $39.95

Size: 8 1/2" x 11" 168 pages hard cover
over 200 photographs
ISBN: 0-88740-448-0 $29.95

Size: 8 1/2" x 11" 168 pages hard cover
over 200 photographs
ISBN: 0-88740-515-0 $29.95